Carolyn

In a few years
the three of us can
do this too!

Joann

LOVERS & OTHER LOSSES

LOVERS & OTHER LOSSES

Poems by Seven Women

Lorene Erickson

Louise Bernikow

Nadean Bishop

Almitra David

Patricia Hooper

Carolyn Gregory

Judith McCombs

ISIS PRESS

ACKNOWLEDGMENTS

Grateful acknowledgment is made to the editors
of books and magazines in which some of the
poems in this volume first appeared: ANON,
BELOIT POETRY JOURNAL, CAROLINA QUARTERLY,
CENTENNIAL REVIEW, CORRIDORS, ECLIPSE, EGO
FLIGHT, EMPYREA, FEMINIST STUDIES, GAEA,GREEN
RIVER REVIEW, HANGING LOOSE, THE LITTLE MAGA-
ZINE, MODERN POETRY STUDIES, NIMROD, THE OHIO
REVIEW, POETRY LORE, POETRY NOW, SEASONS OF
SMALL PURPOSE, SISTERS & OTHER SELVES, SUNBURY
ONE, WAVES (Toronto), WOMAN POET, WOMAN POET:
THE MID-WEST.

Grateful acknowledgment is made for the Josephine
Nevins Keal Award which has made possible the
publication of this volume.

Manufactured in the United States of America.

Library of Congress Cataloging in Publication
Bishop, Nadean, ed. 1932 –
   Lovers & Other Losses: Poems by Seven Women
   I. Title. II. American Poetry--Twentieth C.
   III. Women--Poetry.
                    811'.5'408   81-84364
ISBN: 0-9409-4400-6 pbk.

Designed by Jennifer Spoon

Cover Photograph Collage: "Sad Dreams on
   Cold Mornings" by Joanne Leonard

Published by and available from:

ISIS PRESS
1516 Morton Avenue
Ann Arbor, Michigan 48104

CONTENTS

Lorene Erickson

VISION

In the Men's Department at Hudson's
I choose packages of underwear
and it comes to me in a vision
that another woman in another place
will take them from you.

You will bend to her
and her arms will lift the shirt over your head
like a great sail. Her hands
will slip under the band of brief
and ease them down. Her hands
will map old swales, curves, inlets,
the path of spine, buttock, shank, knee,
an unmarked foot or hand, the porch of an ear,
all places to harbor.

Her body will be like my body, with subtle
shifts of difference.
Her skin and the land under her skin
will be different.
Her eyes will be new compasses.
Her thighs will open in common gesture.
She will cry aloud and moan, or not.
She will know less of you than I know,
and more, for with her,
you will be some other man, giving
what you believe is all
you have to give and enough.

This vision comes to me
and I take my purchase, knowing
that when you come home from that other place,
you will call me into a communion of arms
and tell me what it is like to love.

LETTER

Your right hand under the table trembling
holds the line of a letter
you cast to another address, a hook
for another woman's hand.

My look stops you with your hand under,
neither there where memory keeps
the slow tremor of her body,
nor here where breath falters.

When your hand lifts, finally, for air
the letter is a white sea
you slide into your pocket.
"I'm thinking of a poem," you say,

Sounding a need for words,
and you lie your way into a poem, hoping
a metaphor may lead you back
to the pulse under her skin.

I wait for these rhythms to sink
into language, limn the delicate distance.
In my real and present bones, I wait
for you to catch my face with full hands.

WITNESS

I dream that no one wants you.

You bring a woman to our bed.
She is dark-eyed, dark-haired.
Not me, perhaps my sister.

You ask her for her body,
not for keeping, only
for moments of close attention.

You reach for her, feel
her flesh turning from you.

You fear there may be limits,
that the white heat you've lived by
is passing out of you,

that, soon, you may not want
the bloodfire, may not even
remember.

You are mine,
my father,
my child,
my lover,
my body.

I must take you in,
honor each breath
against the certitude of ice,

keep your desire luminous
in the pitch of my dream.

SWEET INDIFFERENCE

You turn the pages
and your sweet
indifference creeps
upon me like a sickness.
I become a compulsive eater.
I chew your hair.
Threads of it catch
between my teeth.
I lick your nostrils,
eat at lips and chin.
The solid crunch
of your fingers
resounds in my skull.
I separate
and crack each rib,
suck the marrow
and gnaw
the soft, pulpy ends.
My tongue surrounds you.
Your blood swells
my mouth.
No part of you
escapes me.
My jaws ache.
I wipe the last
running juices
with my hair.
I reduce you to table scraps
fit only
for stinking dogs
and scavenger beetles.

You turn another page.

YOU LOOK

you look at him
with the love you look
at him with the love in my eyes

you touch him
with my fingers you touch him
feel his heat as he leans
you lick your tongue in the curve
of his throat   I taste the salt

he does not know
it is me he breathes
he sees another body   yours
your hair nesting his hands

when you press him to your breasts
your belly   press his head
between your legs   he remembers
he remembers only the dark moment
knows only his own cells spinning

we are not a part of him
we are the hundred hands stroking
the eyes looking

LEARNING THE OLD NAME

It was on the main street of town
in an old car full of young girls laughing
running fast burning gears racing
the pack of boys in high blood
windows rolled down on summer night breeze
drying fever shuddering to a halt
at the light

It was only the tease never the promise
adventure driving us through liquid evening
desperate for love for attention
wanting to give in to crash against bodies
against steel glass another metal
deeper more violent than speed

street colors bleeding past us
unable to stop unwilling to stop
for the hands waving us over off the road
waving us into what we wished for
more than laughter

When the words from that boy sliced the night
of my sixteenth year becoming.
"You're nothing but a piece of shit!"

It was enough to doubt.
A marrow poison to carry in us always
to make us sensible and small
and woman.

MARIGOLDS

Marigolds.
Mary's gold.
Lucy's gold, too,
for she planted them every spring,
indestructible
clumps and masses of gold
tinged with red,
full beds of them by the back door.
Sometimes we couldn't shut the screen
without crushing them,
that acrid odor filling the hallway.

The cancer cells bloomed
like marigolds.
Her body smelled like marigolds.

They last a long time when cut,
two weeks, two years,
filled with blooming cells,
hair spread across the pillow
like marigolds.

TO LIVE WITH WOMEN

Autumn
and I think of the time to live with women.

I see them, gray heads
in pairs
leaning through supermarkets
behind quarter-filled pushcarts.

They are the regulars,
arm in arm
in first-Friday bank lines.

I see them in Sunday restaurants
squinting at separate checks,
counting change

companions,
the ghosts of their men long diffused,
the smell of a man washed from their sheets
for twenty years or more.

I see those ladies
gusting toward another winter
buying K-Mart wool to knit afghans,
orange and purple for distant daughters,
yellow, too, for snapshots of great grandbabies.

They know
they will survive awhile together,
those old women.

It is autumn.
I think of what I must do
about the house, the family,
to prepare for snow,
another hard season.

I wonder what early star to watch for,
what smell in the air,
what overnight changes in the grass
and leaves
and me.

What connections must I make
to prepare for the time to live with women?
What friendships must I nurture
to grow into the light beyond
mother and wife?
What women will wait the time with me?

Who will root with me
through seasons of small purpose?

Louise Bernikow

THE WAY THE YEAR BEGINS

Simple removal of a shirt and the way
You watch. Nothing now is innocent.
Ten years stitching my life to your life,
Separation and calamitous
Change. The way I loved you torn, called
Treachery, exorcised, stamped out,
Ashes threatening to re-ignite against
My will. I am afraid of the fire.
I am afraid of the way you watch,
Coldness of the day, rattling window panes,
Coldness of the light and what the
Calendar says: First of The Year,
Mythology of Fresh Starts.
A shirt falling to the floor,
But nothing is innocent.
Ten years of violence, war, shuddering
Of winter months and deliberate
Indulgence of summers. I have walked
In the wind with your voice at my back
And hidden in bed for months.
Sometimes I have told you the chronicle
Unfolding, then forgotten you
And now I stand shirtless before
A trembling window and a new year.

All that was left of domestic things
Was one poultry shears and hate,
Rising, like temperature, on days of
Least resistance. Other men I have thought
Better than you, then changed them in the dark
To resemble you. One whole decade.
What we have in common is loving
And murdering each other,
Night after night,mothering/fathering
Each other, weeks of suspicion,
Potential children lost in menstrual blood,
Wanted, not wanted, the poles between
Us a clothesline hung with dirty linen
And the dream of spring's airy sheets.
Later I will know how you hovered
At this moment, but I see you now
Moving toward me, your hands reaching me
Before your heart does, your arms
Lifting me in ancient ritual.
Shirtless in the cold a year begins.

LA SAGRADA FAMILIA

I rode to Chicago beside a woman
Soon to follow her husband
To an Arab land where she
Had no friends, who said:
"But I never complain"
And crunched peanuts between her teeth.
She had a divorced daughter and
A new thought about marriage:
"Don't do it," she said, "and don't,
For chrissakes, have children."
I saw you at the end of the corridor
At O'Hare, leaning on a white post,
Waiting. "You know," she said as she
Squeezed my arm, "In spite of everything,
I still believe in romance."

Three days. Two nights. I never saw Chicago.
I thought of Gaudi, his Sagrada Familia,
Unfinished cathedral, the façade now rubble
Where Barcelona's lovers leave condoms.
In your bed in Chicago in a dream
You walked down a road in Spain
Stepping over stones, calling me
To follow. There was red wine on my forehead
And the corners of my mouth. A cypress
Bent over you. You said,
"Leave me alone. I want to walk alone."
Later we lay together somewhere near Fez
Me on my belly and you, familiar by then,
An old friend, shivering, came into me
And fell asleep on my back.
When I turned over, we were
In the Atlas mountains making love
On a snowbank surrounded by beggars.
I never saw Chicago.

Later I grew fuller breasts, a swollen womb.
You said, "Abortion. What's the problem?
Now it's easy." I know.
Arab women do it alone with needles and knives.
I think I will take a trip to Spain,
Squat in that abandoned lot, bleed
All of Chicago into the rubble
Of Gaudi's Sagrada Familia.

Poet's note: La Sagrada Familia is a cathedral
in Barcelona designed by the architect Gaudi.
The only part of the building ever constructed
is the façade. The words "La Sagrada Familia"
mean The Holy Family.

LETTER TO AN UNKNOWN LOVER

I have landed you wait, forehead stretching toward me
I am walking backward what if I want to go home?
Last night the women of my family sat on folding chairs
Speaking of disease after disease, amputation of breasts
Demolition of wombs, cervixes in half a dozen cities
Freeze-burned the cursedness the cause
                              of screaming women.
This has brought me to you I have landed you wait
I am walking backward into 1955 and boundless loneliness
The single sailboat on a lake full of ice, trying
I am trying to believe it is still possible in 1977 that
We be railroad cars sidling toward one another,
                              that whole
Selves can couple and remain whole
                    until the lights go out.
Last night the women of my family sat on folding chairs
Pretending it was 1955 and my body was virgin and you
Were the dream of the future, the solution and the goal.
This has brought me to you Resistance, doubt and rage
Roll along on the handtruck They unload the luggage
I have landed you wait with the fear of death
That wakes you every morning at six and your memories
Of hearts broken so badly the bodies that carried them
                              died
Waiting A chair is waiting in the circle of chairs
The women expect my return my collection of trophies
Tell me now here at the landing tell me
What is possible in death's debris the ruins 1977?

SUSAN'S MADNESS

She left in the morning
Drinking the dew
Sent letters back
In yellow crayon,
Was mad
Lost touch
Sipped truth
From green bottles
Jailed herself
In the moon
Made love
To minotaurs
Kept diaries
In code
Left in the winter
Never returned.

SHE HEALS ME

She heals me, this woman
Full of scars
Down from the mountain
Who shivered when the sun
Went down and
Held me, a woman
Full of tears
Told me a story
Of bleeding eyes
A woman, this woman
Full of the stars.

CANCER IS NOT A POEM

People dying of cancer are not writing poems
Mauled by pain, bedraggled in hairless dreams
Descending from hearty darkeyed women playing
Poker wearing perfume never-staying-home to
Eighty pounds in a hospital bed begging
A hearty darkeyed granddaughter to please to
Please bring her something to end the misery
And darkeyed daughters of grandmothers dead
Of cancer wait decades to write this poem

People dying of cancer are not writing poems
Praying in California sun holistic healers
Never happening losing breasts to the ready
Knife and bravely getting tattoed on the spot
While hearty darkeyed friends remembering grandmother
Pray no harm will come to you no harm
Will come to urine-sodden sheets and eighty
Pounds at the end of your life

People dying of cancer are not writing poems
In Oklahoma towns a boy who loves boys
Whisks strangers to motel rooms riding shame
Double in the night, the hidden cancer and
The hidden sex, making a terrible connection
Between them and the local boys don't know
His name or that he is far from home

People dying of cancer are not writing poems
On Hubert Humphrey's grave nor saying what
In Minnesota wormed its way into the body
Beneath the heroics the slow multiplication
Of death carried in Minnesota's air the hero
Carried in state in terrible silent state

People dying of cancer are not writing poems
About the decay of marriages although I have
Seen the impotent rage in marriages dying
While one weds hopelessness and the other
Is dying of cancer and breathing despair

People dying of cancer are not writing letters
to congressmen or to you not marching not
Shouting not bombing not rebelling not
Shaking their fists at the pestilent air

Heartless, inviolate, the pestilent air
Disguised as a lover, plants its insidious
Caress on grandmothers lovers California
Oklahoma, is really a rapist, the air
Invades lung liver cervix breast bladder
While the Muse recoils in dizzy horror
And hearty darkeyed poets tear their own hair

IN THE PALACE OF LAHORE

(for Honor Moore)

You and I, what would we have done here,
jewels among jewels in ruby-walled rooms,
gazing into our mirrors, reflections
reflecting faces, stones, the cupped ceiling?
What, in the bath, proximity of
shining backs, naked arms, strands of hair
floating in the pool, would we
have whispered and would there have been
secrets in our emergence from blue water
to warm stone, crossing the courtyard,
dressing, again, enclosed by rubies,
winding our bodies in gossamer cloth
threaded with gold. Would there have been
secrets in our shuffling back and forth
to the blue mosque, huddling together
in turquoise robes? How much, as the sun
crossed the sky, would we have attended
the coming and going beyond our rooms,
the fall of empire and its belligerent rise,
councils of strangers, horsemen at the gate,
the raised silver sword? What would we have woven
of narrative, epic or lyric
these late afternoons, eating the Emperor's
bread, dry, flat, laced with sand of the city?
And when the red had gone out of the sunset
and we had come to the cushions, carpets
of the Emperor's bed and lain by his side,
what would have come back at us from light on glass
moving beneath the arches, what mosaic
conception might have shuddered as candles
shook in the evening heat? You and I, veiled,
chimes in our speech, returning to our rooms,
lit by one playing candle on tiled walls,
what affinities, what treacheries,
what humid thoughts would we have dared?

Nadean Bishop

TWO WITH A TAUT ROPE

In <u>Women in Love</u> Lawrence allowed as how
A bad love swallowed you up; and no one wants to be
Devouring dragon or hapless Pinocchio in whale belly.
But in a good love, two equals have a rope between them.

I see us roped as climbers, conquering the glacier:
"Watch that soft spot in the crust," "I've got you,"
"Cuddle here in my warmth while we watch the sunrise
Sparkle on the snow," "Plant that flag on the peak."

Sometimes our rope's a jumprope, sustaining whirling
                              dervish playmates,
Dancing and spinning and tumbling laughing in a heap,
Or chanting together in rhythm while twirling for some
Jumper between us: "One, two, buckle my shoe."

Once the rope was Indian lasso, lashing us chest
                              to chest,
While neighborhood hoodlums war-whooped around us.
We slipped the loops and turned them into bull-whips,
Chasing the warriors back across the dusty lot
                              to mother's skirt-tail.

Other times the rope was twine woven between us two,
Matching hands picking up the loop for cat's cradle
                              beauty.
How we held our breaths to reconstruct
That masterpiece from common string.

Suddenly today on the phone you dropped the cradle
                              in a tangle,
Kicked the bullwhip behind the cat-topped trash can,
Tore the bell off the jumprope and plopped it
                              forlorn at my feet,
And without warning as the sun turned crust to mush

Dropped me down the closest crevasse.

FRAMED

My wire frames wafted themselves away.
Remember, I slipped them off as we lay
Before the fire and later toyed with them,
Uncrossing the bows, as the alchemy
Dissolved our crossed wits and tangled
Together our feelings, warmly shared.
Fond of fingering smooth metal I played,
The eyepieces unneeded for our kind of vision.

Today as a workday began I searched
The mantle, the piano, the bookcases,
The floor where the cat knocked the books.
Dismantling the couch, frantic, I saw
The crumbs and dust under the cushions, nothing
Of what I needed. Then I pushed down the springs
And suddenly a cavern opened and my hands
Reclaimed lost treasures of ten years: pens,
Letters, scissors, pencils, my amber necklace.
The shock was dizzying. My cuddling couch,
Revealing a long pouch of stolen goods reborn.

I called you to share the wonder and you wondered
If I'd gone mad, interrupting routine for domestic
Discovery. I wish you would return my gold rims,
Remove my vision from your vest pocket as you
Removed our mingled bodies, spirits, from your mind.

ERADICATED

KoRecType me out of your schedule, will you?
And Liquid Paper me out of your date book too?
Incinderate six months of your diaries and then
Untape my name from your mailbox. No clue, so when
Your new love comes calling and lolling by firelight
No echo of me will come through, till the night
You sprinkle the crystals I bought you in Paris
On birch logs sawed in tandem at daybreak to harrass
The kids in the cottage next door who caroused till four,
Clink our Bermuda-bought Waterford goblets and kiss
As you pour our Amoretto di Saronno till you score
In the mist of the gift of JOY I left. You miss

Nothing.

DANCING DOLL WITH SCISSORS

I only meant to snip the strings, marionette master,
Why all the blood?
To do the dance you drilled me in, undone.

I only meant to see if we could be as good unbound.
Why all the blood?
To be me, free, loosed from your tangling tree.

My Pinocchio nose grows, I lie.
My shears were aimed for your jugular, you die.
I crumple, then rise to dye my dancing feet in your blood.

A PSYCHOLOGIST TALKS
FAR INTO THE NIGHT

Get this--in three years' time nineteen I knew
committed suicide. Nineteen people I knew
well enough to sit down with for an hour's talk--
lost. And that's the way it's put, you know--
lost. Not "A patient suicided on me." O no,
but like he/she won, I lost.

                        The one I lost
walked in and said to Dave and me
"I'm going to commit suicide," and we said
"Would you like to talk about it?" and he said
"No."
        He went over to the Arb and took
a lot of pills--180 dexedrin or something--
and left a long note about how
the mosquitoes were **biting** his feet.

It was a rampant bloody epidemic.

The staff would romanticize it and build it up,
so the patients, to be successful, would have to go
through with it. And we'd get together and say,
"Isn't it awful?" and "Who will be next?" and
"Something horrible is going to hit."
We knew it and we couldn't stop it.
The staff were like carriers, but three
of them did it too--one gently with head
in oven.

                        And I got so
I couldn't get out of bed. Five years and $20,000
of psychoanalysis later, I still don't know
I'm whole enough to go back into practice.

A FLEDGLING DANCER DREAMS

In the dream my sweet Christian mother
Did what she never did in life:
She showed her age and her rage.
My dark lush sister, beauty queen,
Got yelled at: "You slut!"
It was an echo of Mary Hartman
Telling the nuns about Heather,
But it came into my mother's pure mouth.
"Giving yourself to that divorced man.
How that wounded me!"

I was standing off to one side, grinning,
Feeling like the kid I was when she kissed
Him on the couch while I curled in a chair
With a book, peeking at their passion. But
In the dream my grown-up sister said
Straight out to my mother: "I'll never
Regret that--he taught me so much."
I loved her for the courage that took
And felt better about chewing the ear
Of the missionary's kid in the dark car
Riding home from seeing "The Red Shoes."

As the dream unwound, the family went to a play
That was real and we were real and the ballet dancer
Took a pistol out of her Isadora Duncan drape
And handed it to the placid father, who quickly
Put the barrel in his mouth and blew his brains out
All over the dress of Isadora. Mother sobbed
Until I comforted her with my arm around her
And with my soft cheek against her greying hair.

AFTER CHRISTMAS AT THE GUGGENHEIM

Curving in swoops around Mondrian and Picasso,
Mocking the mods in clichés and fancy spoofs,
Tossing jibes to be regrown, lurching in safety
Down to "We're closing" and 11° and furred hordes
Stalking busses by Central Park and me saying
"I want to stay until Monday with this going on"
And you nodding and wanting and joking about the
Golden Ball dropping in Times Square and then
The hug close and meant and no kiss though meant,
Me mouthing, "I love you" where you can't hear,
                                        but see
And then just me, alone, loving you, and you,
Alone, walking to wait an hour for your therapist
In a warm office, alone. "I like it there," alone,
Because the world is bestial and ugly and
Frightening.

JUST LIKE DADDY

Today, at forty-three, I first drew smoke in me,
My inner space invaded with Winston's warmth.
The furry feeling tingled at first,
Stimulating nothing but a memory
Of my father's breath, his stubbly chin
Against my sleepy child's face. That took me back
To a picture of myself at four, defiant
With chin out, in Daddy's hat with Daddy's pipe
And labeled in Mother's careful backhand:
"Just like Daddy." How proud I was.

In those days I bought candy Camels
With pink tips and strutted with my friends,
Playing liberated lady before crunching them down.
Today my moistened lips respond as to a kiss.
I inhale and get no surge or shock, only
The suffocation of a crammed committee room.

Now an hour later my nostrils know I've fallen
                              from grace,
And my frail father coughs toward the grave.

LINES FROM GAIL'S WEDDING

My daughter glowed as she strode down the aisle,
Exchanged the vows solemnly,
Then turned to speak her poem.

"Death stalks me," she said.
"Death knows me and has tasted me
And been left wanting."

I choked up, remembering
The ten-years-ago terror, her body
Dropping a pound a day, the colitis
Eating the ulcers deeper and deeper.

"I know parts of me have already been eaten
                                        by Death.
I see the ragged edges of the bites," she said.

Mother of the bride, elegant in green velvet,
                                    I coughed,
Intruding on her moment of truth-saying to Don
Before God and these witnesses.

"When I am with you," she said,
"I don't have to run, I am safe, I am home."

I cried. She has made it free.
She has found that other home.

"You have healed my wounds,
Driven the ulcers from my body," she vowed.

I smiled, wanting her home and safe and healed.

THE TWO TOGETHER

(A found poem created out of phrases in sequence from
entries entitled "Orchestration," "Orfeo," "Organ,"
"Organ stops," "Glissando," and "Organum" all from
The Harvard Brief Dictionary of Music.)

To achieve the desired effects
Within the limitations, rhythmic punctuation,
For climactic effects much more freely,
In a much more prominent position than formerly,
The beloved sets out to recover her.
Touched, cannot resist her insistent pleading.
Transported to Paradise, the lovers may be reunited.

Each organ has its own specifications.
They must be used only together.
If properly used are among the most valuable resources.

A very difficult virtuoso effect
A simple sliding of the hand produces.
A great body, greatly admired and imitated.

The principle of a vibrating tongue
Which beats against an opening,
An epochal innovation.

Patricia Hooper

OTHER LIVES

Some days a road streams back, a road you took
past someone's house: the porch propped up with boards,
the car dismantled in the yard, a door
where half-dressed children watch you with a look
you'd save for God. They're someone else's kids,
distant as someone else's needs and rent,
the life you never wanted if you tried.

Or it's a train you're riding: past a field
you catch a glimpse of someone hanging clothes,
long days you dreamed of, and she never looks.
Or it's a town where boys grow up to leave:
the two of them, still joking near a store,
stall like a sepia photograph, a scene
glimpsed in a 'forties movie that's run out.

Some nights you wake to this. In every house
on your own block, dark speaks with different names.
A door slams shut, dogs bark, your neighbor coughs,
a car drives up and leaves. The night's the same,
and yet its worlds are different, worlds apart.
You dream of rooms. You enter someone's life
some nights as though his heart beats in your heart.

READING A POEM

It
happens when
the weather
shifts suddenly or
someone kisses
your throat
or you enter
a certain room
from your childhood
the same
wallpaper   old
clothes   gusts
stirring the curtains
Things
let go   And you
stand there
you can't leave
and you
don't say
no

IN SUMMER

Hot afternoon   July
choking the lilac branches
And underneath
we spread our picnic   Kool-Aid
and sandwiches on a quilt

Maybe we told secrets
or watched stuffed-animal clouds
shifting their tails and faces
Maybe it grew late
and after we lost your nickel
and shade crept up the grassblades
one of us got called home

After dinner you went
to your grandmother's or I went
to play in my bedroom   It got
dark   leaves
stirred at my screen   I slept
close to the window and when
your door slammed and the lights
went out upstairs in your house
I wanted to tell you: I am
here in my room   I feel
this breeze on my skin   I can see
where your house is   I cannot
see what you see   And even
if you stayed in my room you could not
be where I am ever   I am
here

POEM FOR A CHILD
SEEN ONLY AT NIGHTFALL

At night the child with the hump
went into the neighborhood
where most of the downstairs lights
were already off, and grass
darkened in long stretches
toward the black rose-garden.
She walked slowly, and no one
came to a doorway except
to close it, although she startled
and rushed from under her old
enemy, the streetlight.
Then she traced mounds of alyssum,
fingering stars as the blind
learn borders of lace. And her mother,
whose other children were sleeping,
watched trembling at the window.
She felt how the fates were holding
the criminals far off
and the red dawn hung suspended
over another country.
A few hours and it would be
filling a long schoolroom
with fire-haired boys and pointing
straight at the luminous hump-back
of the girl in the front row.

THE PARK

I take my mail to the park.
While my children are playing, I read
letters, one from a friend

who tells me her child died.
I read it again. It is like
news from another language

which is not known here.
In the park, children are playing;
their shouts rise like balloons

or kites, skimming the oak trees,
sailing aloft for hours
through spring's tremulous blue.

Yet I read on, barely seeing.
No words, but these hieroglyphics
of anguish to be deciphered

slowly: <u>as if a tiny</u>
<u>invisible star exploded</u>
<u>at the base of his brain</u>. . . . The children

race to the drinking-fountain
just as I notice the trees
in this park are glass. They are shedding

razor-leaves, intricate pieces
on edge in the path. I crawl there
on my bare knees and my hands.

THE WINDOW

The field drifts into darkness.
From my window I make out
the edge of the porch, no further.
Finally, the stars regather;
unmended, the moon moves forth.

Night after night I've seen it.
Drying the dishes, or scouring,
I've looked up, in my kitchen,
and noticed the sun dissolving,
flame after flame, into cloud.

Into deep, fathomless blackness.
They say that the stars are leaving
vast holes when they perish. I need
no evidence, but believe this
earnestly. As I study

black glass for a trace of road,
it is as if the table
and the voices from bedrooms, even
the walls of the kitchen were severed
behind me, from where I stand

staring out into infinite absence.
And I think, Let something be out there,
a fox or a deer. . . . In daylight
deer stood in the field. Now I see them
in memory, standing attentive

at the row of birches beyond
the path to the barn. They will not
come closer, although I would ask it
if I knew how. If I knew
the way, I would summon a road

and a lamp further off, a window
where someone stands squinting at something
believable in the distance.
Then I could believe the barn
and the deer at the edge of it, even

my breath on the glass as I move
past the moon into emptiness, stars
going dark in the universe . . . drifting
like an astronaut, clutching these lifelines:
this towel, this plate in my hand.

9:00

Waking up late this morning, in full sunlight,
I hear your voices already down in the kitchen,
trying to find the cereal, telling a joke
you've already told, and water faithfully
                                running,
blessing the ceremony. Touching the cupboard,
touching the plate, or each other, we touch
                                something
invisible, like a secret we almost remember,
which earth hints at. Quickly, I touch
                        the blanket
as if in an ancient ritual, taking on texture
and strength from the threads which were once
                        animal-fur.
If I woke in heaven, I'd say <u>wood</u>, <u>bread</u>,
                        and your names.

PSALM

It's not the sun
making the day sacred.

There have been other days,
brighter, and less holy.

There have been mornings
as clear, and with no pain

of being, no sharp joy.
And if the sun

has a transparency now,
how could you feel it

were it not for the leaves
illumined to that clarity,

the white table, the rushes
by the road, in the pond,

and the jay's body, its flash
among elms, clattering branches,

each carefully telling you
what it knows about light.

THE LANDSCAPE OF THE USEFUL

Living a long time
in the landscape of the useful,
earth-colored houses
and brown yards springing
with vegetables of little odor,

she sometimes heard
how the birds sang far off
in fields, and the carnival-
bright dawn came, clear yellow

in the kitchens of other women
who were still dozing.
Their white lace nightgowns
bloomed on the spring clotheslines
whole Mondays;
if questioned, their brief
glances could draw blood.

Almitra David

UNBURYING MOTHER

1

with only the tip of the spade
I probe
I am
afraid to push the earth
there is the possibility
of worms   I don't
want to cut flesh

when you rocked me
your fingers stroked
my forehead
I watch the earth
split
my fingers are white
gripping the spade
my fingers are
white as the flour on
your hands
kneading bread
you rubbed your hands together
I hear the gritty sound
this dirt is dry
there are webs of roots
I don't recognize
didn't ask
while you rolled out the pasta
or pinched the edges of the piecrust
I never asked what
was under the kitchen

2

my weight shifts
leg to leg
the veins in your legs
ink
spreading wordless
if I asked   you said
"only at night they throb"
when I reach you
I will massage your legs
you will tell me of
when you danced those
Saturdays you slipped
past your mother's bed
without her calling
Anna . . . Anna . . .
do you know Anna
if the morning star were
still called Ishtar-Inanna
no crucifix would have hung
on your bedroom wall
no selfless Mary would have
smiled at your self's death
Anna   how you would have danced

3

I've hit rock
pacienza, pacienza
you would say
nobody's born with it
not like feet arms eyes
pacienza
useful in prison
nuns call it a virtue
sometimes at night I think
I have it   I say
now that the sun has set
I have it
but my hair sticks out
and my clothes hang crooked

I'll move these
rocks with my hands
rocks heavier than
your two babies
dead after birth
heavy as the doctor
who would not cut
who said do it alone
you'll feel more like a woman
you'll feel more

now the earth
gives under me
the third time he relented
after all, it wasn't Abruzzi
it was Pittsburgh
and 1941 was modern
was softer than
the limestone that
never moves in Abruzzi
he relented made
the incision like
god splitting a mountain
letting water rush
spilling over his hands
my head in his hands

4

now the sun warms
my shoulders
the digging is easier
you rubbed my back
asked was I
cold hungry tired sad
did I need
now I need
to tell you

when you left I was
in the middle of a sentence
my voice lost
in someone else's sound
like a pebble dropped
into someone else's sea
now I know
our words
the ones you hinted
with your eyes   your hands
I know our words
the ones you made into
bread for supper
the ones that never
spoke of your hunger
I feel the sun on
my shoulders soon
we will eat together
we will have
coffee and warm anise bread
and the words will fall
from your apron
from your lips   your eyes
from your thick gray hair
loose and wild
the words will fall
and we will dance in them
and laugh and cry in them
hand in hand two women
we will crumble our silence
like this dirt
relenting
beneath my feet

ON THE ROOF

                ". . . Has she sunk
                root in yr watering place, does she look
                w/her wolf's eyes out of your head?"

                        Diane di Prima, *Loba*

1

I awake here: you say "sleepwalking"

every morning
the same old definitions
startle me

awake   I climb
the open stairs to
this place

here I meet Loba   we
leap from roof to roof   when I
first met her I said
I am not a hunter
and she laughed   I said
I have always believed
there should be no prey
and she laughed
so her teeth
dripped the moon
and I put my hands
round her throat and
choked her
you can see
the bruises on my neck
here   just under
the pearl necklace you gave me

2

sit here   remember
the kettles and
brooms of the Mayans   how
they flew against
the walls
feel the pull of things
away from this house
a shoe   a spoon

sit here   (if we were higher
you would see)
these houses   small enough to
play with   small enough
to toss into a box

3

like my skin I
know this house
where the doors are
what spots
not to step on
I know the
length of the hall   the turn
to the bedroom   the rough
places on the wall   how many
steps from wall to
smooth sheets

I know the way to the roof

do not mistake
my pacing for
indecision

4

today the rainspout pours
lost words
back into the earth
I cup my hands to
catch them
a taste takes me
back to a table of
fruits and flowers   back to
my words   the ones
stolen and broken
the magic ones
the chants and prayers and songs
the ones damned and
called unspeakable
the words I need
to name my hunger
my pain   my love
all are here
rushing
by me

5

I am thinking of roofs of
sun-colored clay
earth on the roof
temples on the roof
I arrange
clay pots of begonias in
pink and red circles
I make moons of
white-flowering trefoil

here I wait for
whispers   for wind
for the White Goddess who
sometimes   just before light
brings me seed from
the flowers that grow wild
around her temple

GEORGE: SOME OBSERVATIONS

1

if I say "some"
he will ask
"how many"   and I will
remember when I
ran to his books
to find his answers

today it is raining a
September rain for my
birthday   I have
invited him to
come without his
dictionary   but he says
"undefined is unloved"
and I haven't   clearly
defined myself   he says
he despises
clouds
September or not

2

he comes
with a list of the
sons-of-bitches and bastards of the world
he pronounces each name
and says   "repeat after me"

he watches my mouth
to see if
I'm saying it right

3

after he puts his Hemingway and Dugan
and Berryman back on the shelf
he says   "life is shit"
and   "get me a drink"

even in May he says
"life is shit"

4

bitterness is
unbecoming
in women   he says

5

last year his wife noticed
that all the measures were off
for instance the one-cup measure
no longer felt familiar in her hand
and she knew
she couldn't tell him
that the earth had shifted

George went on believing
the steps were ten inches wide with
one-foot risers   she didn't want to
confuse him -- he
walked those steps in his sleep

only yesterday he had gone to
survey the basement again
"our house is safe from floods" he said
she thought she might say   the earth
has shifted   but

he had put his glasses in his pocket
and his chair was still comfortable

Carolyn Gregory

EDEN

Perhaps today when the jay routes
messages to the flock,
I will take leave of my senses,
bury the body like a moldy shirt
and enter the waving grasses,
never to return again. Equinox,

when the lilac thickens
the city disappears
and all the faces of men
bathing in greed stop.
In woods, on this route,
I'll drop all the beggar's slogans.
The universe of parallels emerges
quick, like green, itself, across the stream
where vines braid old trees
in gentle partnership. After a time,
I follow the compass of wind
and will not leap today
into the grotto, dark like infinity.

Change is inevitable.
May revises its mood
when the creatures require it.

I look before I leap.

Past dogwood on soft needles,
lovers gather their petals
as dust scatters lightly.
Friends speak softly, dreaming
of the apple tree above the crickets.

Remedy for death exists
where the land is not stubborn
with purpose. No journal does it justice.

Stirring, all words gather like wet
leaves when we gambol over stumps.
Even wood grows red with sap
kindling with the grasshoppers.

At the river robins name,
set all baggage down. Let the river
save you for the hundredth time.
Clouds and homunculi live
on the same earth where
mud poppies and crow
share their golden island.
Even when dust rises, birds sing
their aves, just before the sunshower.

After hours, all the bones gather here
as the living dwell in former springs.

You cross your heart
In this chapel of sense.
Young girls laugh, gathering swampgrass
when you score the length of days
as the moonlight lingers
over this pool, made from the rhythms
of grass and wings,
tuning these invisible strings.

ST. JOAN

Nights in the stone tower
the jailer rolls the door in place
after the tray of food disappears.

"I turn toward a square window overlooking
this world of fields and plowmen,
small as bees beneath gray sky.
I grow big with desire
like a woman in waiting.
Breasts swell with the heavenly child
rocking among stars.
Though I cannot touch myself,
I burn a hundred feet down
to the small pit of cells
the cross of heaven and earth begin.

"Night is my jailer.
It stirs snow through wind
with songs to hush my soldiers.
War flashes and sputters
in a city more distant
than the mother of flowers,
waiting for her child to come home."

ATLAS

When it snows, she carries the world's weight
on her shoulders
as though underground holding the roads
up for travellers.
She is not buried though
alone, she wears a small red bonnet
so the north
will not make her suffer ice
and tracks of hungry animals.

The whole dark winter is her coat
filled with brambles and millet
from the silence
where a river goes, isolate of the lowland.

And when the others tell her sad tales
of lost empires, they hold cups of coffee
on the corner.
She tilts toward them,
the sound of heavy axles slipping
over earth.

OFFERING (FOR DIDO)

Day and night would accept you,
opening the heart
to bless with the food
natural colors bring.
Angel, soar high.

Never die, broken from miracles
the tongue inspires
with its memory of bread.
No sin, no fear can disinter
from the arena of stars,
letting you inside the skin
to sit and draw the crayon wish
children never lose.

Come home and sit in the sun.
I will brush webs
from your breast,
stir love after a long voyage
on the ship you dreamed
mutiny for years.

Let us be the partners of our bodies.
Three bells call us now.

CANDLES

Evening after words and women cross hands
in the wood room,
incense burns bright around the willows.
I burn a candle in memory
that writes "speech after a long silence"
in my book.
Leaves are the wet children of a nurse
gone away to darkness.

The gold skin goes away to clouds
you say I must pass to enter heaven
but faith suspends in broken leaves
like the skeletons of footsteps.

Day's names make the candlewax of night.
I smear them in my skin
to turn away cold
whose sparrows turn in nests
the gold falls through.

In a quiet room, the light is failing.
I turn up the lamp
by the rhythm of the wind
and say this prayer.
Each letter holds a fire
like a candlestick
I can live by
and be strong as the girl-child
growing deep inside the night.

OTTILIE'S BIRTHDAY

(for Ottilie Hermann Miller, 1886-   )

There is some sign hope triumphs here
after the sand castles of youth
go down where anthills leave
in another season.
On Ottilie's birthday, bells ring
past her golden wedding, the gate
opens to a path of blue stones
and lilies
where great grandchildren
skip and sing. I used to play
Alice Blue Gown under her apple tree.

On Ottilie's birthday, rain is sweet
like old valentines grown
yellow as the primrose
brought from the mountains.
I remember paintings redolent
with rose cherubs
dancing in a ring,
her spring birthed over
and over again
or how we nodded with the
china doll in Brooklyn's attic.

Little, long ago, she would rock me
in her tree house
near the fire crackling green
and sing as the lake frogs hummed
all the tales of fairies and
impossible wise men.
As I moved into the knotholes
of sleep,
electric storms crackled
on some other hill.

Grandmother, you were the shadow
of the Christmas angel,
gold above the lake
in Saratoga dusk.
You were the road from the crayfish grave
all the woods pitched us to celebrate.

Each swing in the fragile moon
heaven and earth drew us natives
closer, closer to this June.

THE DARK WOODS

When you went away,
you stole the feather pillow
after kicking her between the ribs.
You carved the path to the house
for fifteen years.
She was the same property
your will took in
like the fat cow and pasture.
Obedience made you preen
like a common rooster.

Each day, before you left
another mark on the wall
cut your passage from the grotto
of silence.

Even in August,
dry grass stiffened
where you plotted an "x"
to sink the body, unwanted
as dead starlings.

You shrugged when
the matter is you have
no love to give
for love drives no new fences,
and cannot polish the boots
you use to walk farther
inside your own dark woods.

Judith McCombs

THE MUSCLES OF LOVE

Who would miss the soul if it left,
and the body survived? Who would notice a loss?
Who can divide spirit from breath?
Before you took body, child of my body,
you were no one: the muscles of love made you live;
your eyes made you see. And who would abstract
trust from your sleep, your fingers from kneading,
your mouth from its hunger and love?

I think that my soul looks out from my eyes,
the joys that I know inhabit my flesh,
my prayers, such as they are,
meander the lobes between this ear and that,
are locked in the curious bones of my skull.
There is love in my fingers, love and my work.
I am no one outside of this body.

Therefore I will praise it, and cling,
like a child to the mothering thighs,
as it shrivels and sags, as it dies in my hands.

A PROSPECT OF FLOWERS

(for Freud & Joyce)

Swinging the tassel
of my Mexican belt,
not thinking, just playing,
I upend the floppy pompom
and find myself nuzzling
the flower revealed--
petals of yarn
touching my nose,
a hard bud-knot in my lips--
I remember the babe,
improbably pink,
who lolled in the center
of an overblown rose
on my Mother's Day card--
I think of the children
poking their heads
through the narrowest opening
of the sleeping bag,
giggling and crowding
together like flowers--
does he think of flowers
when he opens my body
to nuzzle and kiss?
How strange if he did,
how pleasing, how strange
that would be.

THE NIGHT CHILD

In the six o'clock blackness, just before supper,
in the dark winter rain, the child is running
from Kimmie's to home, leaping & bounding
through the glittering backyards, past unlit basements,
singing Whooey Whooey An owl or a dragon
rushing through darkness
The face in her furry brown hood
is a strange shape swooping toward me

Behind, at an angle, Kimmie's tall mother
stands at her screen door, a black silhouette
looking out from the yellow light of her kitchen
Ahead lie the glistening alley, its potholes
brimming with blackness, & another backyard
& her own mother watching, black against yellow
As she rushes & leaps through the shining night
like the last of the spirits calling itself,
like a creature trying its strange new wings,
it seems that the glistening sidewalk is a tether
we have allowed her, & the alley a gap
where we cannot protect her

& I wish she could stop in this singing, still singing--
not take me into her song, that's too much--
but if somewhere in the back of my dreams, or memory
she could always be rushing & leaping toward me
like a wild dreaming bird, come at my call,
mysteriously gliding on her feathery song

Now she enters her own yellow kitchen, stomping,
complaining   I hug her, my wet furry friend
of the night She's too squirmy to hug "Guess what
We had push-ups & Batman at Kimmie's So there"
& she bounds up the stairs to wash for her supper
singing Whooey Whooey
                        I am glad I could dance
like a moth in this warm yellow kitchen, remembering
her darkness

THE SISTERS

In my head is this picture, remembered:
two women in shirts, sitting alone on a beach
watching a stubby brown kid
shovel the sand and the water
In my head I can see
the sullen slump of the women's backs
they are stranded
grownups washed up in the middle of nowhere
stuck with each other
watching the kid
as it dibbles the sand or spatters the shallows
a squint of envy/unease/something else in their eyes
they are stranded
creatures washed out of their shells
flabby ripples of white at belly and thighs

What is wrong?
this is the good life/comfort/
                    a thousand full-color advertisements

Now in my head the image comes closer
the voices, the words move into range
I see through the eyes of one of the women
 I didn't want to be her but I am--
she is too old, not eager enough
a thick bulky door is shut in her face
her arms are too heavy, holding her down
she doesn't believe that heroes are coming
today or tomorrow
she doesn't believe in heroes/rescues/herself
therefore no heroes will come
which is all her own fault
for dreaming wrong dreams

How do I get rid of this woman?
she squats in my clothes, sullen, disgruntled
an overgrown child I cannot evict

The younger, my sister,
keeps looking away from the woman I am
her hands are busy, shoving the sand,
pushing and smoothing it over
she talks and I listen
what should she do with her lover?
she doesn't want motherhood yet
she blames the women
on the Israeli commune she tried this summer
they sulked in the kitchens
wishing for cities/apartments/TV--
why weren't they out in the sun
plowing the desert, grabbing the crops?

Would she want me to follow her out to the fields?
how could I ask for myself/for the women
I am soft from my kitchen
my options are gone, washed away, sand among sand

In the dark of my head I see
my sister turning away from the woman I am
her face shuts down, her eyes stare hard at my kid
she wants to get moving, she isn't stuck here
but her fingers are smoothing the sand,
                         smoothing her belly
her eyes are hungry/angry/alone
I remember my fingers smoothing my belly
cradling the head of the child in my womb

My sister/my child could turn into me
we are women

IN THE YEAR OF HIS DEATH

In the year of his death I drove North
alone, with only the child that was there,
no one inside me. Road drifts & darkness,
coming in too late to the wilderness cabin--
the bay iced over, the track through the woods
ice over mud over ice, the low car
slewing in ruts, no place to stop--
why was I there?
                        In the year of his death,
at the Northernmost spine of land before water,
the old trail to the point flooded over, half-ice,
not safe with the child. In the bowl of cedar
between bay ice & marsh, where no one could see,
the animal's skeleton, headless, brass casings
inside, around us the silence. The child
gathered the pelvis & blades of its shoulders,
made masks for her face till I stopped her
     touching his face at the viewing,
    Why is he painted like that?
I didn't say why.
                        In the rented cabin
the skull on a shelf, a candle inside,
souvenir from the hunters or gatherers before us.
The woodpile wet ice & wet pulp, I couldn't
stop shivering, in thermals, in down; the bad tooth
broke off in my mouth. Deer tracks by the pump,
ice shouldering old ice out in the bay,
why was I there?
                        Packing out to the car,
the child balked in the drifts, I panicked
& had to keep going, I didn't know why,
there was nothing but silence.

HOW IT IS

By the chute to the hallway incinerator
for these many decent & quiet apartments,
at the end of this empty Sunday morning,
sit the elderly indoor slippers of dark morocco
from someone unknown, someone not here,
woman or man, of woman born,
all stuck with the same cold shins at the end.

I think of the briefcase my colleague left,
thrown out with his notes, after the stroke;
of the downstairs widows, adjusted or not,
each doing her pittance of laundry, alone;
of the man who lay staring, thrown from his car,
dark-eyed at the edge of some childhood road;
of the aunt I loved best, not there at the end
of the long-distance phone my father answered;
my only father, who is also not there,
not anywhere now.

Though the garbage I bring each morning is full,
through the fire roars snugly in the furnace below,
though I have my own to get back to, those warm
& noisy young bodies, whose feet I remember
climbing inside me, whose feet will keep climbing,
year after year, out of my reach--

I think how it is--
                    what does one tell them?--
when someday sure, thinking or not,
these feet will be going, like it or not,
skinny & cold, as all feet go,
left right at the end of the cold stick shins.

THE INHERITOR

September, & these cold hill streets where the Quakers
failed & died out. Beside the old road
spirea goes grey, goes bald, & the tame
barberry argues with gusts, claws
at the cold, useless as grief. Overgrown,
dying back, ivy billows & tugs
at old mortar, old walls. High overhead
blue sheetwinds of cold race for the South,
for the warmth, for the glaring great hill of sand
where my father lies dead & dead indeed
under heaven. Here shelter draws into itself,
crumbles like mortar. Here the great burial hill
pulls down its toothless stones, though the hands
on these soft Quaker tablets point upwards to heaven.
Here memory trails out, useless. Upright
against the cold I push the bundled child
of his bones, child of his eyes, child
of the year of his death. At the crest of the hill
I kneel & hold the bundled child
to warm my hands. Below, the empty
trees, the tame hill streets; the cold
earth falls away. We living build
on hills of sand, on hills of shifting clay.

BIOGRAPHIES OF THE POETS

Louise Bernikow is well known as the author of several books of prose, most recently AMONG WOMEN, an exploration of the varieties of women's relationships with one another. The editor of THE WORLD SPLIT OPEN, her life as a poet is closely tied to the feminist movement. She gave her first poetry reading at a political rally in the late sixties and she has found that her poetry is intimately related to her political and intellectual passions. Support and inspiration came, in large and generous doses, from the late Muriel Rukeyser. Louise Bernikow lives in New York City, where she is now engrossed in writing an historical novel and travelling to college campuses to lecture on the subject of women and literature.

Nadean Bishop is a poet, professor, and lay minister who received her Ph.D. from the University of Wisconsin-Madison. She is an Associate Professor at Eastern Michigan University, where she served as Coordinator of Women's Studies for three years. She contributed chapters to THE AMERICAN WOMAN: HER PAST, HER PRESENT, HER FUTURE and WOMEN: A FEMINIST PERSPECTIVE, and has recently completed a book manuscript of oral histories entitled GRAND-MOTHERS AND GRANDDAUGHTERS. As Michigan Coordinator of the Feminist Writers' Guild, she has given poetry readings in San Francisco, Milwaukee, Ypsilanti, and Ann Arbor, and her poems have appeared in ALURA QUARTERLY, CONTEMPORARY LITERARY REVIEW, CORNUCOPIA, CORRIDORS, ECLIPSE, and POETRY LORE. The divorced mother of four children, she serves as Lay Assistant in Campus Ministry at the University of Michigan for American Baptists.

Almitra David lives in Kutztown, Penn-
sylvania, and teaches through the continuing
education program of Cedar Crest College. Her
poems have appeared in the BELOIT POETRY
JOURNAL, POETS ON:, STONE COUNTRY, CHOMO-URI,
EARTH'S DAUGHTERS, 13th MOON, and PLANSWOMAN,
among others. Her translations of the Argen-
tine poet, Alfonsina Storni, are in the 1981
international issue of CALYX. She is a member
of the Feminist Writers' Guild and Poets &
Writers, Inc.

Lorene Erickson poet, educator, and writing
consultant, grew up in Detroit. She received
her B.A. and M.E. from Wayne State University,
squeezing classes in between full-time work
and full-time family responsibilities. She
taught in Detroit and Livonia Public Schools
for eleven years and was named Michigan's Out-
standing Creative Writing Teacher in 1977.
She is currently teaching writing at Washtenaw
Community College. She has given many readings
and has published poems in small press journals,
magazines, and anthologies. Her first book of
poetry, SEASONS OF SMALL PURPOSE, was published
in 1980.

Carolyn Gregory was educated in New York
and at the University of Michigan where she
studied with Robert Hayden. She has coordin-
ated workshops and poetry readings in Michigan,
including the Guild House Regional Poetry
Series, Poetry in the Park, and Rhyme Space,
and has done numerous readings in Michigan,
New York, Massachusetts, and Colorado. Poems
and critical essays have appeared in PRIMAVERA,
GREENFIELD REVIEW, MOVING OUT, WAYNE REVIEW,
MIDWEST POETRY REVIEW, GOOD COMPANY: POETS AT
MICHIGAN, WOMEN'S POETRY ANTHOLOGY, CORRIDORS,

CHETTAS: A CHAPBOOK, and others. She lives in
Boston and plans to become a minister in the
Catholic Church to do work for human rights.

Patricia Hooper was born in Saginaw, Michi-
gan, and received her B.A. and M.A. degrees
from the University of Michigan where she was
awarded five Hopwood Awards for poetry. She
taught for several years in the English Depart-
ment at Wayne State University. Her book-
length manuscript was the runner-up in the
Yale Series of Younger Poets in 1980 and was
a recent finalist in the National Poetry Series.
Her poems have appeared in THE OHIO REVIEW,
POETRY, CHICAGO REVIEW, THE AMERICAN SCHOLAR,
THE LITERARY REVIEW, and many others. Her
poems were awarded a SOUTHERN POETRY REVIEW
prize and the 1980 Ames Award from the Poetry
Society of America.

Judith McCombs   is an Associate Professor
at the Center for Creative Studies College of
Art & Design in Detroit. Her first book SISTERS
& OTHER SELVES was published in 1976 and AGAINST
NATURE: WILDERNESS POEMS based on backpacking
experiences appeared in 1979. Poems from her
third book manuscript AMERICAN GOTHIC were
awarded the second Neruda-NIMROD prize in 1980.
She has published poetry, fiction and essays
extensively in journals and anthologies. In
1971 she founded MOVING OUT, the nation's
oldest surviving feminist literary journal.
As a Writer in the Schools with the Michigan
Council for the Arts, she specializes in visual
and narrative poetry. She has done many
readings and in 1981 began visual performances.
After receiving two grants for visual production
from the MCA, she mounted a three-week show en-
titled "Disintegration Series" in No. Carolina.